A Bird in the House

12.25.19

To Jane + George + Max.

It so good to see you

again.

Let's find each other

in the Napa Valley!

Much love,

Ann-Marie

A Bird in the House

POEMS
Anne-Marie Cappellano

DRAWINGS
Mark Cappellano

LOS ANGELES, CA • 2018

ISBN: 978-1979348799

Drawings by Mark Cappellano, Instagram @cappellanoarts
Front Cover design by Jonathan Schute
Book design by Pablo Capra

Contents

Drawings

Acknowledgements

First, I want to thank Madelyne Bailey, whose delight and encouragement was all I needed in those early years. I'd like to thank Paul Leslie for his elegant and keen pencil editing, and Alden Marin for mirroring pure inspiration and creative courage. You are a blast of color and light in our family's life. Thanks to Evan Hartzel for first publishing my poems in his online magazine, *Brackish*, followed so elegantly by Laura Alvarez in her blog, *Clothes Stories*. Many, many thanks to Pablo Capra for all your focused work. You helped make such a beautiful book.

And truly, without Sanda Jasper and her sneaky plan and devotion, this book would not exist. Thank you so much for being my guide out.

Lastly, LOVE to my patient husband Mark and our girls, Nina and Delilah. You have torn my heart open. Thank you for allowing me to write about our life together.

Burrowing Owl

An Introduction

I love to write… which should be pretty obvious since you're holding my book and one would hope there was joy involved in its creation. Yes. There was. Writing gives me tremendous energy, makes me a better parent and a happier, funnier, smarter person. I believe it even makes me look better and (oddly enough) enjoy music more.

But writing has also caused me despair and even agony. Even though it's what I've wanted to do most in my life, I've experienced a lot of resistance without understanding why.

Writer's block is not everyone's problem. Many people I studied with in college and in writing workshops are published novelists and produced screenwriters. Yet others who were equally talented (if not more so) have disappeared. Writer's block is very painful if it goes on for too long. So is writer's shame. Often these days when I tell people that I'm publishing a book of my poetry, many say, "I write poems too—but I'd never publish them." When I ask if they'd share them with me, they say, *No, no. No way,* and escape in a plume of embarrassment.

So I want to tell you how I have overcome writer's block—about the very scary, creepy nature of resistance and how clearly I see the role it has played in my life until now. Now just about every weekday I wake up and write. It's not quite a habit like making my coffee, but it's a close second. This book may not seem like much… *I'm self-publishing. It's pretty spare. What's with the birds?* But little accomplishments in one person's life can be huge victories for others—and this has been huge for me. So maybe I also want to write this as a reminder to myself. I have come through this madness, and I can sure as hell do it again.

Okay, so here we go. I'm going to start at the beginning:

I have found that there are three different places one can be stopped when writing. **Place One** is before you even start. You're charged with good ideas, ideas that can add to the dialogue of our times, entertain, help or even heal. But you don't do it. You just don't write. Everything stays up in your head and you just wait for the right time, but that time never seems to come.

This first place has not been my biggest challenge—I write impulsively, obsessively because I have since I was a kid when I found it helped me out of anxiety and dark moods. That being said, it's a wicked double-edged sword because just writing (on pads, in journals, on scraps of paper found in the kitchen drawer or in the Notes App of your phone) doesn't get you very far (except therapeutically) if your intention is to be a professional writer.

So **Place Two** is to write but to not finish anything. That's where my true "issue" comes in and has *stayed* for most of my adult life since college.

When I was younger I finished my writing projects. I had to. I was in school. I wrote plays in high school, then in college I wrote more plays and comedy sketches, then, catching on to the hipness of the film world, I transferred to USC and wrote screenplays. When I graduated I was given a big writing award and a job at a very important production company. I was sitting pretty.

But after a series of difficult events, (a hard break-up, the LA riots, the Northridge Earthquake, my parents divorce, and finally being crushed by at least three auto-immune disorders), I lost my way. These events didn't suddenly make me a bad writer, but I lost confidence in myself and stopped finishing anything I started. To make matters worse I became a critic! A "Reader," which was a popular job that production companies gave to starting out screenwriters. I would read and summarize other's people's scripts for a small fee—over and over again. I knew something was very wrong when I eviscerated the screenplay of the movie, Erin Brockovich, then sat in the theater two years later watching this beautiful, strong character driven film unfold in exactly the same way I had read it. I kept thinking, what the f—k is wrong with you, Anne-Marie? I was 27, growing more snarky by the day—and going nowhere in the film industry.

I decided to change course—which to this day I can rationalize was the right idea. Thanks (…or maybe *not* thanks?) to an inheritance from my grandmother, I became a hospice volunteer, got a Master's degree in Spiritual Psychology, got married, became a mother and then moved to the Napa Valley to plant a vineyard and make wine with my family. Not too bad, right? Not bad at all… unless what you really want to be (also doing) is writing, publishing or making films. By the time my daughters were in middle school and I no longer had the excuse of being to busy, any energy or fight I had to push my writing projects through to the end had evaporated. So I paid people or schools to force me to write. That didn't work either.

Part of me knew that even if I started writing a story again, it was bound for the pile of papers at the back of my desk, or hidden in Word files in my computer. Determination mixed with despair does not get you very far.

I was so frustrated and so mad at myself. I was also very busy and I could use that as an excuse to the outside world—but not to me. To make matters worse my health was deteriorating even more. I would wake up, get my girls off to school then crawl back into bed. Afternoons brought me tension headaches. My hormones went haywire and I had an allergy to just about every food and air-born molecule God has put on earth.

Oh come on! Who can live this way?

I finally stumbled upon a great therapist. I'll spare you my weekly analysis by cutting to the end: Fear. It was fear. Sheer, cunning fear. If there is evil in the world, it's fear.

Fear is most often what causes resistance and writer's block and it was causing mine through constant self-doubt. Fear freezes, makes you look the other way, or run the other way. But what on earth was I so afraid of?

First off, I was afraid of not being good enough, and then of being humiliated for not being good enough if I shared my work. This fear was like a door that faithfully kept my self-confidence out—to protect me! Only it was cruel because it would open sometimes and let a little confidence and creativity stream in—then shut just as fast. How did I get here, I wondered? My father is an architect and an absolute by-the-book-perfectionist. He had to be. The only time he was ever sued was when the roof he designed on a modern house was slightly off on its angle—causing it to drain badly, causing leaks and a pain for the client. It really shook me because his client had become his friend, and I was shocked at her punitive reaction. Yet my father understood. There is no room for mistakes when designing a house. He drew the plans and gave those plans to the builders who depended on his rightness and his skill.

But for me as a creative writer? What did perfection mean? I think my greatest fear was to be criticized by someone "like myself."

And here was the shift:

I could see a sort of glimmer in my therapist's eyes. "Hey, why don't you just write me some shitty poems? They can be *really bad*," she said. "No one will read them but me, I promise. Bring some in".

… Poems? I never thought of poems. I guess I could do that. She's so nice. She would never judge me.

So I started writing these *shitty poems*. Freely. I wrote about walking the dogs, agonizing over snacks for my kids' classes, the mothers of these kids, my own mother, my father, then my sadness and frustration.

I started calling them my *shadow poems* and boy, did I let loose! I would bring them into therapy, read them and just cry. I can't tell you how much I cherished these sad, sweet and most importantly—*finished* poems. I would print them out, put them in a decorative folder and carry them around with me while running errands and driving my girls. If I had a moment while waiting in a dentist's office or in carpool, I would open the folder, read them and my heart would sing my own personal anthem, filling the doctor's office or my five-year-old Toyota Highlander with magical stardust fairies who adored me.

Over time, the sadness faded and the poems got better. I didn't need to bring them into therapy anymore. I was actually finding my way into territory and topics I thought I could never express or return to. How incredible! After over *twenty years*, **Place Two** was actually over. By simply finishing a work, it stood free and independent. Who cared that I wasn't a trained poet and had never thought I'd be a poet. I was writing. These poems existed and they were done, baby!

Then I decided it would be a great idea to do this poetry book.

Why not? Put them out into the world. I had worked hard on them. They were sad at times—but honest. My husband and my friends liked them.

Enter **Place Three**! Yes, one can be stopped at the very end, when it's time to share the work that has been finished. Why not? Fear is opportunistic. It doesn't care where the party is, it just wants to go and slam doors.

As I gathered my poems for the book, a whole surge of fresh terror arrived. Throw them out into the world? For just anyone to see? Anyone to ridicule? Are you kidding? They need to be edited, they ALL need to be rewritten.

I found a few people who actually were poets at some time of their lives, and they diligently pencil-edited my work, or told me to start over, or circled one sentence and said, Keep this. This is good.

This is good? this one sentence of a two-page poem? I agonized over these pencil-edits for months, made adjustments, but I couldn't change these poems into new works. They already existed. They were alive and free. It felt like *poecide.*

New waves of resistance came at me. Maybe we need to move. I need to take a meditation class, travel to India. Should we get divorced?

No, Anne. Stop it! Stop right here.

There will be no move. There will be no divorce. There will be a book—I'm doing this!

I don't even care if these poems suck and everyone hates them (or nobody reads them). I am publishing them as an act of Life itself. Because what is the opposite of fear? Yep, it's love. In the end, I have to love myself. Love my process. Love this new beginning and love where I'm going. I would do this for my daughters and this is what I will do for myself—support what I love and what resonates for me, and then keep going even while afraid.

So this is my story—these are the three places I've been stopped and overcome so far. There may be new places along the way and I will have to face those with love and determination too. Because lastly (this is very important), unless you're Eckhart Tolle or the Dalai Lama, resistance from fear never completely goes away. Discovering resistance is like coming across a trap door in your closet and finding a man who has been living in there for a very long time who's sole job is to come up with ways to stop you from thriving. It's creepy how well he knows you, how he's been feeding off your emotions. You shine light on him and shout bloody murder for him to get out—you even yank him across the street where you can see him from your writing desk, but he never leaves.

Be ready. The trick is to know he's there, hold your pen in one hand while you write—and give him the finger with the other. Sit there and finish some "shitty" stuff. Start easy. Something simple but truly honest. Start at your beginning. Or start at the end and then figure out what happened. Nobody starts out perfectly. They have to put in the time and work to get there. They have to learn through trial and error. Work on your creation as much as you can, and then let it go. Then keep going for another day. It's not easy if you are a creative person who wants to share their voice with the world, but it's imperative to your life and your health—so do it.

* * *

I've included some of my husband Mark's bird drawings. This is how he expresses himself creatively while working outside the house as a conservationist.

An avid bird-watcher, Mark taught me to watch patiently for birds through binoculars on our honeymoon in Spain. Poetry is like that—catching sight of something important or beautiful that could be gone in an instant, looking closely for the details. Poetry brings brief moments of clarity, when the indescribable is somehow described—a bird flying through the unconscious, caught and then set down on paper. Not trapped, but observed, lit up, and then released.

The first bird Mark ever drew was late one night when he was very, very sick. He had caught a virus that was attacking his thyroid gland—experiencing what the doctors actually called a *thyroid storm*. It was horrible for him and horrible to watch as all his energy drained out of him. One morning the girls and I came down to the kitchen to

Blue-gray Gnatcatcher *(Mark's first bird)*

discover a bird drawing he had done while we were asleep. We were in awe. It was incredible. Where did it come from? He had never drawn anything like it. It was as if this bird had flown through the storm and right out of him.

And then they just kept coming—a new one about every two weeks—so similar to the pace I was writing poems. Somehow the poems and the birds seem to go together, like gifts given to us by our higher selves—or from the place our creative spirit resides.

These are some of my favorite poems. Lucky for you, I've left most of the shitty ones out.

Enjoy,

ANNE-MARIE CAPPELLANO
February, 2018

A Bird in the House

Whimbrel

This Must be the Body I Chose

This must be the body I chose.
How I love its honest shape.
It fits me.
My face is unremarkable but pretty.
I am not tall but I am not short.
My feet are narrow and not attractive in any way
But they have taken me to the places I've wanted to go.
My soles are flat from carrying my girls.
Toenails that curve up to the sky.
I forget about the gap in my teeth until someone points it out to me.
My breasts are small. My rib cage is small
I suppose I am small although I don't feel that way.
My thighs are somewhat large.
They keep me from wearing skinny jeans
But are my daughter's favorite place to nap.
Knobby knees.
I like my profile. I love to smile and watch people smile back at me.
For now, my body is a perfect match to my soul
And I will tend to her until the day we part.

2014

The Volunteer

I'm the volunteer assigned to you.
The discomfort has finally been explained.
There will be no recovery.
Even though I look you in the eye and smile,
You won't recognize me.
A regular Laura Ingalls
In a button-up blouse, jeans and clogs.
In whatever hospital chair I can find
I'll read to you
The more soothing parts of the Bible,
Some of the Psalms if you want
Or letters from your daughter in Chicago.
You sleep or drift off, hands empty in your lap.

What's going on? You ask me when you wake.
I tell you I have no idea.
We laugh quietly, so as not to disturb the sutures in your heart
But there's something I do know, and don't say:
This dying will be an antidote to how you lived.
You'll finally have to cede control
Or care for yourself when no one else will.
I've seen it play out so many times, in different beds.
You wave your hand in the space between us.
It is round and faded like a battered abalone shell.
Death, what is it anyway?
I decide to keep my wild beliefs to myself.
Maybe you will just leave from where you entered.
You're silent while you consider this.
How could a girl as young as me know anything about anything?
You're right, I smile. I should stop

You'll need me more when they move you to a sub-par nursing home
With just a bed and motel-style bath,
Your monitors underpaid and unhappy people
Who watch soap operas on your TV and hog the remote.
I get it back for you—
Though for all I know they take it right back when I leave.
I hide your purse from them
Between the mattress and the bed frame
Under a pale blue blanket.

In the early morning your struggling heart will set off alarms
But I won't be there when they mistakenly resuscitate you.
And you'll be crankier than ever
Appalled at the weight of the sheets,
At the IV tugging at your hand like a fish hook
This horrible, god-forsaken place!
Where is my daughter, why has she left me here?
Tears burning down your cheeks.
I place my hand on yours and try to pour love into you.
It's all I can think to do.

A few days later your breath has grown uninterested.
I can count ten Mississippi before it returns.
The doctor arrives and prescribes a heavy dose
Of something streaming from a plastic bag.
You will finally get your peace
And I'll go home to an empty house.

The social worker calls me late and tells me
You've passed away
That it will be okay, even good.
Our jobs are done for now.

Three years later I have my first child
And never return to this work.
You may laugh but no one is leaving under my watch.
No one.   *2018*

22

Stellar's Jay

For Mark

Twenty years ago you came into my life
wearing the loss of your father
and the musty smell of a church.
You were cute but too young and my mind said No!

But we found ourselves seated next to each other
at a long supper club table
and talked urgently instead of eating
while the other guests looked on is dismay (disgust?)
In a context I've now forgotten, I used the word *Fastidious*
and you were impressed.
I asked about your relationship with your mother
and I wish I could remember what you said.

After our second date
I was ready to send you off forever,
but standing in the curve of my parents' driveway
you touched my back
and we were drawn—not a quiet arch,
but two electrical currents
discovering their on switch.

Soon you helped move me from my moldy carriage house
into a sun-filled Ranch house in the hills.
By its kidney shaped pool,
we lay next to each other on the warm terracotta tiles,
the boy with the man hiding somewhere inside
the woman hiding the girl grasping your hand.

2015

I Gave it Away

About ten years ago, when the girls were still little,
I gave my favorite poetry book away
to another mother who was also writing.
We met in a book club, but I had seen her before.
Her comments from the starched sectional were more intellectual
than personal. She was working hard on her short stories—unlike me.

Then I saw she published an article in our local newspaper.
It was before blogs, but she had that air about her—
rising with the birds to write before her kids came down for cereal,
escaping to The Mission in her mom car for a class
taught by a semi-retired Buddhist professor or celebrity poet.

That day I heard it was her birthday.
Someone would bring a homemade cake,
an exquisite bottle of sparking wine of their own making.
An impulse led me to my bookcase and I slipped the book out
of my small poetry collection.
After the class and the cake, I gave it to her.

I never forgave myself for doing that.
So strange because I loved that little book so much.
Why did I try to impress her with my Dorianne Laux?
Here—this is the kind of poetry I want to be writing,
but I'm not because I'm taking care of small children,
keeping house, exercising, and trying to have a social life.

Like a dog that rolls over,
I showed her the fuzz of my underbelly.

A few years later when I began to write more,
I searched for the book but it was either out of print
or not stocked by our local book store.
Dorianne, where were you?
Such a beautiful voice, I thought it was a shame.

I don't remember when I began
To call everyone "sweetie,"
As if they were my daughters,
my darlings, my little birds.
I have always loved too much,
or not enough.

Once the internet was really up and running,
I found Dorianne's web page and bought the book again.
I've moved from that town. Lost track of the mother.
But I hope she still likes the book
and even thinks of me.

2015

Great Blue Heron

My Grandparent's House

Depression runs in my family.
It's more like a dullness.
It looks like nothing but feels like less.
People like me can sometimes turn others off—
I seem like I'm judging
but really I'm just scraping at my heart
for energy or interest.

There's a stubborn normalcy to life.
Wine helps my father but it makes my head ache.
Pills help my aunt but I have no prescription for that.
Sleeping helps, but can make the dullness worse.

Luckily it comes and goes,
and I can hide it well from others.

Sometimes I think I see it in my daughter,
and then the other.
A brackish stream moving through the house,
closing doors and letting meals go by unshared.

As a child we were brought to my grandparent's house.
They'd sit us in their small garden or in front of the TV
and leave us there for hours.
I could feel them through the closed screen door,
the low battery charge of the TV changer,
the muffled pop of the cabinet drawers
my father built on a visit home from college.

Finally my grandmother's cat eyeglasses would appear,
a plate of cheese and mayonnaise sandwiches
left quietly on the table.

The *shy* gene, my mother called it.
Where does this come from?
Flat as the Indiana farmland
A cow's miserable life.
So many children no one even notices
when they go missing.

Or worse—
losing four kids to yellow fever in one night.
Centuries of sadness in your bed
and in your food.

2017

Stay

This the life I created from the dirt under my nails,
from the miles of DNA vibrating inside me and all of the places I
    have been
walking this green and angry planet
this is where my path has led me.
Stay
All the materials are here—
an old soulful house, a husband now of many years, beautiful
    unfurling girls.
I have planted my beds with hard won seeds and sprays of love,
God smiling inside me—always.

Don't let the storms that blow through dishearten you.
Don't make everyone's plot your own.
Your job is to love them all—always.
Love them and let them be.

I will stay,
and by Spring I will be rewarded with rose blossoms
sprouting from my fingers
and children who grow up knowing devotion
from the very beginning.

2014

Lust

Something flew out of me.
I'm not sure when.
A magnificent bird
Too large for my rib cage
With colored wings
And claws that clutch like a bad-fitting bra.
It had to escape or it would surely destroy me.
Was it lark? A lute? A thrush?
Something like that.
A suffering bird that I don't want back
Always hungry and ill at ease.

2015

"Mystery Gull"

My Love Keeps Me Here

We grow up along side our kids. We have to!
They are placed in our hands,
precious and helpless.
Here, You said, take them home and raise them up.
How did You know I could do this?
How did You know I would rise from everything that's held me
    down?

I care that they are well fed,
that they sleep in clean sheets and soft blankets,
that they have great clothes that suit them, and music!
Yes, I care that they hear music in the kitchen,
in the car, in their rooms.
I want them to have pets and fragrant flowers on the counter,
and to travel—to swim in clear oceans
and climb mountains and see all the brilliance,
the people and the art scattered across this world.
I want time to sit and listen to them when they tell me of their day,
then enough energy left to put them to sleep at night.

I have risen to this the way I hope I will one day rise to You—
knowing that I truly did the best I could.
For now, my love for them keeps me here,
tied into this game,
even when I don't want to play.

2015

Slippage

That summer in Iceland
everything was made irrelevant by nature.
The landscape pulsed and roared.
You worried obsessively our girls would fall into a volcano
or slip off the Mid-Atlantic Ridge.
So I held tightly to their hands
(or I pretended to because I thought they could handle themselves).
I joked that maybe we should tie them to us with rope—
like the leashes people put on their kids.

During the day we drove, circling the island in our rented white Volvo.
At night we floated in sulfurous hot springs
holding each other and the children.
There were no stars because the sun barely set—
only the hint of the aurora borealis shimmering above our heads.

The last days were a race to complete our circle
and we came together as a magnificent team—
a perfectly folded map, two minute pee stops,
a quick bowl of rich fish soup at a roadside café.
We dashed into the Water Museum, toured a prolific stone collection
that took a lifetime to gather,
ran across black beaches and drove the endlessly winding fiords.
I took a photo just as we were about to head south
and you looked so handsome and clear.
I thought, *This is so fun.*

Then at home I found the emails you had written.
*We are just rounding the most Northern point of Island and are about
     to head south...*

What a beautiful writer you are, she wrote back.
Who me? Yes, I actually do have a manuscript in my desk drawer...
I sat in our bed, my computer agape,
listening to you play songs on your guitar
(I imagined) no longer inspired by me.

Earlier in the year I had wanted more time to be alone,
to sleep more or just stay in.
I wanted you to go elsewhere for entertainment
instead of looking to me.
Was I somehow to blame?

I could hardly feel sorry for myself.
I had thrown a rope far too long to keep us safe.
It was time to get up and pull you back in.

2016

Jet Lag

At 10pm I will get my mind handed back to me
while everyone else is heading off to bed.
They will get their eight hours of sleep
and I will get three
but I will read, and write
and I will solve all of (my) life's problems
free from picking up after others, from cooking and listening.
The hum of the night will charge me like a firefly
and keep me up until 3:30am
at which point I will go downstairs,
eat a full meal and fall into blessed sleep.

April, 2016

I'm Set Down like a House

I'm set down like a house
no longer wandering or searching.
My collections are complete, my closets clean.
Even my tea drawer is organized.

But it's happening again.
The need to move, the upheaval, the search for a new place to live
that is better, cleaner, safer, brighter… Yes!
Who knows… He may be right.
A rolling stone gathers no dust. There's always a better place.

But I am happy here—placed like the St. Francis statue
into the soft rounded
hide-away nook of our dining room.

Or maybe it's not the house, or all the work we've done on it.
Maybe I'm finally at home within myself
and I don't want to move away.

June, 2016

Black-necked Stilt *(juvenile)*

Smaller

When I turned fourteen my mother and I decided
I needed to be smaller.
Our shopping sprees were no longer fun.
I couldn't wear Levis.
Short dresses revealed pudgy, embarrassing knees.
My brother was not being nice about it either.
He called me the Bread-Eating-Brat or Annie Fannie.
My mother took control and introduced me to Jenny Craig.
I was weighed and spoken to, then
sent off with a bag of dry crackers and a plastic food scale.
I also met Jane Fonda.
She was not the long-suffering daughter on Golden Pond
but a banshee in head-band, leg warmers and creeping leotard
ready to teach me to be super small like her,
but also firm and disciplined.
I can do it! I was white, Protestant, female—
we were bred for deprivation and control.
I went along with it for about a month,
but with my third poached chicken breast of the day,
my mouth watered with tears.
Did I really need to lose five pounds? I mean, Dad and my friends
at school were always telling me how pretty I was.

I must have learned something from Jane because
I soon began to vomit up my food (as she later admitted doing).
Ice cream was the easiest.
My mind was so strong I could will it back up with my thoughts.
For about two years I lived in a garbage disposal,
secret stashes of junk and sadness… so much sadness.

But you know the story.
The ups… the downs…. The ups…

The last woman I met was my therapist, Joan.
I got to sit on the floor with her Golden Retrievers,
(two gorgeous beasts as starving and food obsessed as I was.)
We talked about how much I hated my body, my mother and my
    brother.
(His new name for me was Chute because, well… *he knew*).
She explained it was normal for girls my age to gain weight—
something about reproductive organs developing properly.
She told me I was a lovely soul with an impressive
vocabulary for a girl my age.

I never told Joan about the vomiting.

Funny how when I went away to college it gradually slowed
and then stopped.
Everything except this yearning to stay small.

2014

Bigger

I've decided I'm going to be bigger.
It won't be noticeable at first.
I will slow down on the sprinting and firming and pumping.
I will eat more greedily at meals,
bake brownies and lick the bowl.
Slowly I will creep up a size, then maybe another.
People won't be sure—I'll buy new clothes as I go.

At the market I'll fill my cart with organic brown sugar,
potatoes, yams and avocados,
artisanal goat cheese from the Sonoma or Petaluma hills.
It will be a blur of cooking, feeding and eating,
a coating of butter, a crock-pot of stew.

When I hug people they will gasp,
then surrender to my soft chest.
My husband will have his hands full of me.
My children will be happy and well fed.

2015

Creation

My daughter lets her phone go dead
as if to halt the frantic young voices flying at her
or eliminate the realization that there is no one calling.

Peace, loneliness—how close they both can be.
Sisters almost.
One is beautiful and smiling
the other has mascara running down her eyes
and a radish's bun on top her head.

At carpool she is pale and depleted,
curling away from me,
a saddle bug in her seat.
Every day she is growing tall but losing weight.
She is never heard right—never understood!
At home we quietly close her door
and step away.

In our absence it begins:
a collage of a girl from a distant galaxy
or the materialization of a pinhole camera.
On other nights she has paper-mache'd her bedposts,
made a concentrated try at embroidery, then Origami.

By midnight she emerges
for small Trader Joe brownies and milky tea,
then silently heads back into her room.
For years I fought her, *please go to bed*!
but now we don't talk of sleep.

In the morning the house is cold.
I step over the butchered magazines to wake her.
Pens are strewn across her wood floors.
I find a tight pencil drawing of a jungle flower under her plate,
then a sketch of a mysterious high-cheeked boy.

At breakfast she takes sips of my coffee
and smiles against her will.
The universe has come through her,
restoring her for another day of Middle school.

One day her phone will come alive again—
like a stubborn bird from the dead and tempt her out.
For now I will bask in my daughter's aloof proximity,
the fervent quiet,
and the fury of her creation.

2015

Black-chinned Hummingbird

Eastern Meadowlark

Lila at 12

Every day I thank the butterfly's route that
Delivered this girl to me.

Her wanting to help,
To touch my shoulder and hug me,
To cook new recipes she's found on the internet
And keep it clean....
It comes from such a pure place.
A place far away from me
But that I recognize as me too.

I marvel at the organization of her room.
The sharpened school pencils in their cup,
Clothes so perfect for her
Waiting eagerly in the drawer to be worn.

While her temper can shake us like a 7.5 earthquake
In the night (Fists flying, running, slamming doors)
I ride it out beside her. Earthquakes were, after all,
The natural disaster of my own adolescence.

And just as my mother watched my hair
Turn from lemon blonde to brown,
I'll see that butterfly lead her away from me.
But that's not what this poem is about.

It's about Lila at 12—that arresting gapped tooth smile,
The world map above her bed
With all its pins waiting to be pushed in.
It's about volleyball every day after school

And waking up early on the weekends to play some more,
The long letters of gratitude I receive on Mother's Day
And the delighted, punch-happy love she has for her dad.

I know she will suffer.
(I suffered way too much!)
But she can always return to this place,
And thrive.

2016

The Wonder

This was the summer of the bra.
No breasts yet
But still we shopped online, in the stores,
Target. Bloomingdales! Justice!
We were on it.
The slight padding in the cup was the draw.
Such delight it brought both of us.
That little nudge of what was yet to come.

2015

Our Children Chew on Culture

Our children chew on culture.
They scour the Internet
as we scoured the damp parks
and sour grass fields behind our houses.

I've been told that we can learn more in a day
than people a hundred years ago learned in a lifetime.

From the glow in their rooms
my kids wander through doors we can't follow.
We are shut out by passwords,
sucking on the stems of wild flowers
they will never smell or taste.

Who is trampling the soft mink of their minds?
What are they being fed outside my kitchen?

My husband and I worry, of course.
I go to him for peace
for forgiveness
to sleep against—
trying to forget what I have learned
this long and busy day.

2016

I Wait for Her

The house is so quiet once the carpool takes the girls away.
Their rooms are a mess.
The kitchen is splayed like a car wreck
with me its only witness.

I walk away and sit instead,
waiting for my old familiar self to return,
to approach me and embrace me
like the curious lover she once was.

My impatient list of things-to-do tries to coax its
way into my brain.

I reread notes and make some small edits.
She will come. I know she will come.

I am living a life of immense importance—
to my children and husband only.
Oh yes, and to my dogs.
I am fully employed by them all and she… is my part-time lover.
She disapproves of my life but I tell myself
there is nothing I can do about it.
I've been caught, trapped by this impulse of biology.

Children are works of art, too, I reason,
born from my very own material
shaped by intense love and careful attention to detail…

Shut up! You took the easy route,
grabbed at the low lying fruit.

Her anger at me gives me daily tension headaches, sweats and
calisthenics in the night.

> How can you forget our wild nights together?
> The lovers we took, the mad, joyous journals we filled?
> It was only us!

I have had weeks of impassioned writing,
only to be dropped before anything is finished.
She leaves me with nothing but disappointment in myself.

For how long, I wonder, will I be kept hostage like this?
Both waiting for and dreading the day
I will be free again.
By then... perhaps...
even she will have grown disinterested in me.

So I sit and I wait,
listening as the neighborhood construction starts up,
the dogs grunting and shaking their collars,
and the birds dropping their seeds onto the roof of my car.

2016

Red-crowned Parrot

Red-crested Turaco

Friendships like This

Our friendship has ended terribly, unbearably,
at a gathering with our children and closest friends.
She had outstayed her welcome.
I asked her to go.

Even I hear the angels gasp—
followed by her heavy bombardment of my character.
How dare you! How dare you?
You are not worth the attention I have given you.
You always were... unworthy.
I've been stripped, pushed
and abandoned in the woods.

What can I say?
I once adored her.
She was Queen to my Princess,
the big sister I needed at an overwhelming time.
She organized family trips with our pre-schoolers,
lent me her designer dresses and Jimmy Choo boots.
She even convinced me to use my best china
for everyday dinner parties.
Why not? Life is short.

So was our friendship it seems...

As she marches away from me
I am weighed by a heavy umbrage.
I really am awful.
I'll have to return her dresses,
apologize to her children whom I love.
In full agreement with her,

I lull in this bed of musty Fall leaves.

The birds begin to chirp incessantly.
Come back! Come back!
Oh! Be quiet. Can't you see I'm lulling?
More chirping. … I sit up.

Wait a minute. I'm not trash to be discarded…
I'm this china—my own grandmother's forest-green,
finely-leafed glazed cake stand.
Steady, elegant and surprisingly useful!

No… I'm not only this cake stand—
I am the whole forest surrounding
and embracing my lost self.
The birds rise from their tree in unison and return.
(They have done their good work for the day).

How can I explain this to her?
That I am not the things she says I am.
That she too (even when overstepping)
is gorgeous, intelligent and divine.

It's like trying to convince a dewdrop
it's the whole miraculous sea.
Or that she can amputate me like a limb,
but we are as connected as the roots beneath us.

I can't. I can't convince her… not now, at least.
She saw me through the trees and ran in the other direction!
I called out but she didn't return the call.

So, alas, I will have to find my own big girl boots,
rise from this heap of leaves
and gather my new russet skirts,
pull back my dusty hair and make my merry way
on my own.   *2017*

I Have Known You Forever

When we step from this life my friend,
having relinquished the children and the husbands, the work,
all fight and jealousy draining from our tired bodies,
bathed and brightened,
we will see each other again
and we will laugh
and laugh and laugh and laugh.

—2015

Belted Kingfisher

Dad

---

croaking frogs, stars, soft air

It's night
and wrapped in a towel,
I come into the kitchen from the Jacuzzi.
His house is bright even now, with great height.
I can see the stars from the kitchen,
Smell the wood saturated by years of herbs and coffee
Flowers almost rancid from lazy mornings
Reading the *New York Times*
Many cook books open to Osso Buco recipes,
A faded Chinese rug kindly absorbing the pool water
From my dripping feet.

I can see the stars from his kitchen
The way I will one day see him
His splattered skin now a galaxy above the vineyard
His translucent eyes, the moon,
Watching me go on without him.

2018

Beautiful Mother

My childhood is playing out in my dreams,
at the house my father built down a long driveway,
in the light, busy kitchen where everything happened.
It's as if I can reach out and touch my young, sunny mother,
feel the Indian cottons of her wrap skirt
and faded Petit Baton tee shirts.
I can inhale her soft Chanel smell
and even sense my father's thrill at being so close
to something so beautiful.

Green Honeycreeper

The Walk

Sometimes I'm able to write for long stretches of time
without anyone noticing

and I reach the top where the road gives way to wild grass
and sit on a swing to look out at the view.

The mountain is showing herself off to the tangy sun.
Clouds begin to rise and trail like resting arms.

I see a Japanese print. I think of art, of deep beauty—
my own beauty, so new to me now.

It's like watching a rose finally relax into summer.

2017

There is No Other Way

This is it
busy and funny
and at times tense and exhausting.

I'm a bee covered in its honey
a flower doused in dew
an ant working
meticulously through its maze
in meditation,
with a strength that I never knew I had
all rising to the surface
for you, for me, for us.

I swim in this bath of love and duty
walking a path that is right under my feet
always
leading me to you.

There is no other way.

2017

Made in the USA
San Bernardino, CA
21 January 2019